Healthy Lifestyles

PERSONAL HYGIENE
& SEXUAL HEALTH

Camilla de la Bédoyère

Evans

Contents

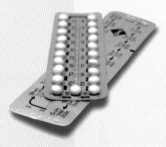

Introduction

When you were younger, it was your parents' job to take care of your health. Now you are growing up, it's time for you to begin taking responsibility for this important area of your life.

Choices for life

Since before you were born, your body has been changing and growing. Most of us hope to stay well for the majority of our lives, and that means following a healthy lifestyle. Of course, some health problems can't be prevented, or cured, but we can all aim to make good lifestyle choices.

DiD YOU KNOW?

You grow from your extremities (hands and feet) first. That's why teenagers often become unusually clumsy – their brains haven't caught up with their new body proportions!

Your body

Now you are a teenager, your body is going through its greatest period of change – adolescence. This time of your life has particular implications for health. As hormones zoom around your body they affect every part, not only making you grow, but causing phenomenal transformations to take place.

Everyone develops at different speeds and in different ways during puberty, so don't feel self-conscious if you're a different height or body shape to your friends.

Dirt can lurk in unexpected places. Mobile phones are a perfect environment for disease-causing bacteria, because they are warm, covered in sweat, and are kept snug in pockets or bags.

The most obvious changes, of course, are the ones that are preparing your body for sex and reproduction. But others that are less obvious take place, too. The texture of your hair and skin may coarsen or become oily, and you probably sweat more than you used to. There are emotional changes as well; you could find yourself being more forgetful, tired or upset. You may have particular concerns about how your body is changing, and how to deal with matters surrounding sex.

Health for the here and now

Many of the things we learn about keeping healthy are to do with staying well and active later in life. Let's face it, it's hard to care about your future health when you have so much to think about today – and being old seems a very long way away. But there are plenty of health issues that affect your body and mind now, or will affect you in the near future, especially those surrounding adolescent lifestyles and sexual health. Equip yourself with the knowledge to deal with them and you may find the whole 'growing up' thing is less painful than it might have been.

Dirt alert

Issues around personal hygiene also crop up around the teenage years as you prepare for adulthood. You learn how to protect your health by keeping your body clean, and you also develop the skills needed to keep a home clean, too – there could be hidden hazards in places you'd never imagined. Scientists have found that all sorts of everyday objects can harbour bacteria, viruses and even parasites! For example, sharing headphones can spread head lice, and computer keyboards are home to more bacteria than a toilet seat.

PUBERTY

Puberty is the time when we go through the physical and mental changes that take us from childhood to adulthood. Girls usually start puberty between the ages of eight and 13. Boys usually start puberty between the ages of 10 and 15. The whole process is controlled by hormones, and lasts for several years in both sexes.

Body Hygiene

You probably thought you'd mastered the art of keeping clean a few years ago. Now your body is going through a transformation, it's time to think again...

Don't sweat it

You have between two and four million sweat glands in your body – and many of them will be in overdrive throughout puberty. There are two types of sweat gland: eccrine and apocrine glands. They have an important function – helping your body maintain a safe temperature. Both types produce sweat, which

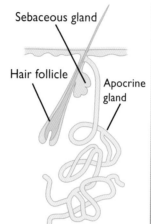

Sebaceous gland

Hair follicle

Apocrine gland

Apocrine glands start producing oils, proteins and fats, as well as sweat, during puberty, and produce even more if you are excited, nervous or stressed.

forms as tiny bubbles at the skin's surface. As sweat evaporates, heat is drawn out of the skin and your body cools. Eccrine glands are found all over your body's surface. Apocrine glands, however, are found next to hair follicles and are concentrated in particular places, such as the head, armpits and groin.

Sweat is just water and salts, so it doesn't have a strong scent of its own. Once exposed to the air, though, bacteria can start to feed on it – especially if it is mixed with secretions from apocrine glands. The result is body odour (BO), and it can be pretty unpleasant for everyone, not just the person who smells!

It's important to replace the fluid you lose when you sweat during exercise.

FEEL-GOOD FACTOR

If you do an hour-long workout you will produce about 500–1000 ml of sweat. Even when you're not exercising, your body is losing water in the form of sweat all the time, so you should drink enough water to replace these lost fluids.

Be a clean teen

Body odour is unlikely to affect you if you wash every day. That means washing from top to toe and paying extra attention to those places where apocrine glands are especially busy and where sweat becomes trapped in dark, dank parts. Always dry yourself with clean towels and change your clothes regularly (underwear daily). Cotton socks and underwear are less likely to make you sweat than ones made with synthetic fabrics, such as nylon or Lycra.

Smell sweet

Even if you wash every day, it is wise to use products that help control armpit sweating. Most adults use an antiperspirant or deodorant every day. Antiperspirants reduce the amount of sweat by blocking the pores that produce it, and usually have a nice smell, too. Deodorants kill odour-creating bacteria and cover any smell with perfume. Never use these products on other parts of your body, especially not your genitals. Some antiperspirants and deodorants can cause a rash, but there are types for sensitive skins.

Many sportspeople develop itchy armpits or groin rashes that are symptoms of fungal infections, caused by excessive sweating. These infections can be treated by a doctor, and a good personal-hygiene routine.

Deodorants and antiperspirants can help avoid body odour.

DiD YOU KNOW?

Doctors can prescribe Botox® treatment in cases of extreme sweating. Botox® temporarily blocks the chemical signals from the nerves that trigger sweating.

BACTERIA

Have you ever wondered why a damp towel quickly develops an unsavoury smell? The whiff is a sign that billions of bacteria – and maybe mould too – have made a home in your towel. Dirty sports kits are also a haven for disease-bearing micro-organisms.

Body Hygiene

You can buy waxing kits to use at home, or go to a beauty salon to have your legs waxed.

Hair everywhere

The hair on your head may have begun to darken, changed its texture, become coarser or even developed curls you never had before. It has probably become a bit greasier, or more unmanageable. These problems can be solved with regular washing, trips to the hairdresser and the use of the right hair products. But what about all that other hair that's sprouting?

Girls

There is no need for women to remove any of their body hair, but many do so for cosmetic reasons. Removing underarm hair also helps to prevent body odour. There are various methods of hair removal, such as shaving, tweezing, depilatory creams, sugaring, waxing and epilation. You will find which one works best for you by experimenting – but always follow the instructions provided to avoid damaging your skin, especially on your face.

WASH YOUR HANDS!

Dirty hands and nails can spread diseases, colds, food poisoning, internal parasites and diarrhoea. Wash your hands after using the toilet, after coughing or sneezing, before preparing food and eating. You should take about 15 seconds, and use hot water, soap and a nailbrush.

Boys

Boys develop darker, coarser hair during puberty – and lots of it! Where your hair will grow, and how much of it, depends on your genes, so if you come from a hairy family, you know what to expect.

In general, pubic and underarm hair grow first, facial hair next and chest hair, if you get any, will come towards the end of puberty. Facial hair is removed by shaving and you can choose dry shaving (with an electric razor) or wet shaving (with a razor and foam, cream or gel). Never share a razor with someone else, to prevent passing infections.

Wash your face and hold a warm wet facecloth to your beard for 30 seconds. Cover your beard with shaving cream, gel or foam. Sweep the razor along your skin, following the direction of hair growth (go with it, not against it). Use light and gentle strokes.

Diseases like athlete's foot are easily spread without proper hygiene for your feet!

Neat feet

Cheesy feet are a common problem: think of all that trapped sweat and billions of bacteria making a home in your shoes. To avoid the problem of foot odour:

• Always wear clean socks, ideally made of cotton.
• Change socks every day.
• Avoid wearing the same pair of shoes or trainers two days in a row. Give your shoes time to dry out and don't wear shoes or trainers without socks.
• Wash your feet thoroughly at least once a day and dry them well.
• Use odour-eating insoles, talcum powder or foot deodorants.

• Go barefoot at home as much as possible (unless you have a verruca or foot infection, and only after you've washed your feet).

Athlete's foot is a fungal infection that usually occurs between the toes. It causes skin to peel and itch, and it is easily passed from one person to another. You can buy treatments for athlete's foot, but good hygiene is essential for any treatment to work effectively.

Body Hygiene

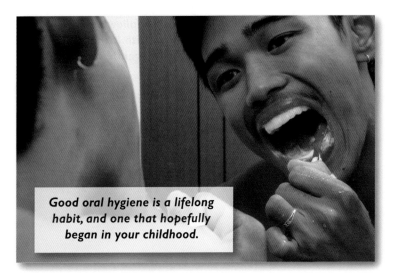

Good oral hygiene is a lifelong habit, and one that hopefully began in your childhood.

Watch your mouth

Here is a fact that may surprise you: a healthy smile is often ranked as the most attractive physical feature a person can have – more important than eyes, hair and body. Despite this, though, many adults pay little attention to their teeth and gums, and end up with painful cavities and abscesses, gum disease or even false teeth. To keep your teeth sparkling, follow these tips:

- Brush twice a day, with fluoride toothpaste.
- Change your toothbrush every three or four months.
- Floss daily.
- Visit the dentist regularly.
- Avoid sugary foods and fizzy or sweet drinks, especially between meals.
- Eat a healthy diet with plenty of fruit and vegetables.
- Don't smoke.

FEEL-GOOD FACTOR

Battle bad breath by using a mouthwash after brushing. Chewing sugar-free gum is also helpful because it increases the amount of saliva in your mouth, which kills bacteria. Drink plain water after meals to dislodge trapped food and remove any sugary substances that encourage bacteria. Smoking and drinking alcohol cause bad breath.

Braces

Many teens are faced with the trauma of orthodontic work to straighten their teeth. Thankfully, the technology behind braces has improved dramatically, so they are not as noticeable as they used to be. There can be considerable discomfort to cope with, though, especially when the braces are new or if they have just been adjusted. Your dentist or doctor can advise you on the best medication to take if you have pain. Your orthodontist can supply soft wax that reduces the pressure of the wires and brackets against your gums.

People with braces do not need to eat a special diet, but they do need to be careful about what they eat. Hard and crunchy food can snap wires or dislodge brackets, and very chewy or sweet food can get stuck and may cause tooth decay. Orthodontic work is normally complete within two years, but patients may be given retainers to wear at night for many years afterwards, because your teeth can continue to move until you are well into your forties.

Piercings

Oral piercings may be fashionable but swelling, infection, pus, bleeding and chipped teeth don't make for a cool look. In fact, oral piercings can be life-threatening; a severely swollen tongue can block the airway, and an

Try not to feel self-conscious if you need braces – you'll be glad you did when you have beautiful teeth as an adult!

open wound in the mouth is a gateway for bacteria to enter the body. For example, oral bacteria that enter the body via gum disease or oral piercings may head for the heart and cause endocarditis, a potentially lethal disease.

Professional piercers advise their customers to be prepared for healing to hurt, and take several weeks. They recommend avoiding caffeine, smoking, alcohol, swimming underwater, chewing gum, sharing cutlery or glasses, drug use and alcohol mouthwashes for as long as the jewellery is in place.

WISDOM TEETH

Wisdom teeth often erupt during the teen years. You may not have room for them, especially if they come through at an angle and put pressure on your other teeth. Dentists use X-rays to work out whether wisdom teeth can stay, or need to be extracted.

Oral piercings can cause all sorts of health problems and should be taken care of properly.

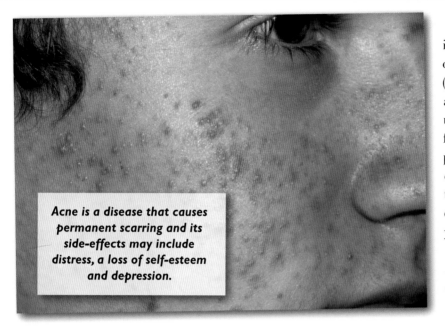

Acne is a disease that causes permanent scarring and its side-effects may include distress, a loss of self-esteem and depression.

Acne is not curable, but it can be controlled. Creams containing benzoyl peroxide (which kills acne bacteria) and salicylic acid (which unblocks pores) can be bought from pharmacies without a prescription and can be very effective. If over-the-counter treatments don't work for you, don't suffer in silence: see your doctor for advice and stronger medications, such as antibiotics, which tackle severe acne.

Break-out!

It's a cruel truth that just when you start to really care about your appearance, and your self-esteem may be a bit shaky, spots and acne break out. During puberty, your skin's sebaceous glands produce extra sebum – an oily substance. This traps dead skin cells so the skin's pores become impacted, allowing bacteria to grow and cause the skin condition we call acne. If your parents had acne, you are more likely to get it too.

YOU'RE NOT ALONE

Spots affect almost every adolescent at some point, and around four in 10 need treatment from a doctor. Acne usually begins between the ages of 10 and 13 and lasts for five to 10 years. It is likely to be worse in males, but females are more likely to see their doctors about acne.

ACNE – FACTS

- *Friction makes acne worse – so tight clothes, or shoulder and chin straps that rub, can cause a break-out.*
- *Cosmetics and moisturisers can make acne worse.*
- *Girls' hormones often cause monthly break-outs.*
- *Like any disease, acne can be made worse by stress.*

ACNE – FICTION

- *Acne is not caused by eating greasy food or chocolate.*
- *Acne is not caused by dirt, but washing your face can help keep it clear of dead skin cells, sweat and excess sebum.*
- *Sunshine and tanning will not improve your skin's condition.*
- *Squeezing impacted spots (they look like large red swellings) won't get rid of them. It pushes the infection further down, causing more damage.*

Tattoos

Tattoos are permanent marks made into the deep layers of the skin by filling a wound with ink. It is essential that tattoos are carried out by licensed practitioners in hygienic surroundings, and that directions for aftercare are followed diligently.

If you are considering a tattoo, check you are up to date with your immunisations, especially hepatitis and tetanus, and talk to your doctor first if you have any medical conditions. Tattoos can affect your immune system, so if you have any allergy problems, eczema, or want to dye your hair – now or in the future – tattoos are probably not for you. Because tattoos are permanent, removal is expensive, time-consuming, painful and it is not guaranteed; it is likely you would still have scars.

REAL LIFE

'I grew 14 cm in six months and got huge red stretch marks on my back. I was really embarrassed, so I told my mates I was attacked by a lion when I was younger, and they believed me! The marks faded quite quickly, and I'm not so bothered about them any more.'

Miles (18)

Think carefully before getting a tattoo. Remember – it's something that you'll have for the rest of your life.

Look Good, Feel Good

How you present yourself to the world will affect all areas of your life, from relationships to work and play. Good presentation also helps to improve your self-esteem.

Body talk

The way you dress, how you stand and the efforts you put into your appearance are all forms of non-verbal communication (NVC). Dressing in a certain style, for example, may be your way of telling others that you belong to a certain friendship group, or follow a particular band or fashion. Maintaining your personal hygiene so you look and smell clean is a form of NVC that is normally considered at the very least to signal politeness and self-respect, as well as respect towards other people.

Check your non-verbal communication. What does it say about you?

It doesn't matter whether you go for grunge gear or prefer more conventional couture – the fact that you care about your appearance and make an effort does, however. It's worth bearing in mind that we all have to change our appearances to suit particular circumstances, such as attending meetings or interviews.

Dress to impress

Looking your best isn't about wearing the most expensive clothes, or visiting beauty parlours; you don't have to spend money to be well-groomed. Often the best turned-out teens are the ones who've used their imaginations and some creativity to put together a look. Simply add a good diet, fresh air, exercise and a dose of confidence – and you have the recipe to turns heads.

OVERCOMING SHYNESS

Everyone feels self-conscious from time to time, and being shy is normal, especially for young people. Acting confident, even when you are not feeling it, can fool people into thinking you have more self-belief than you actually do, and it can become a habit that helps overcome shyness.

You don't need to dress expensively to look nice. Just be clean, tidy, stand up straight – and smile!

It is not so different for humans. It is natural for adolescents to preen, pamper and pose – it's part of learning how make oneself attractive to others – and it is an activity that goes on all over the world. Take a walk down an Italian main street on a warm summer's evening and you will find yourself caught up in *La Passeggiata* – swarms of young people appear, dressed up and looking gorgeous, and stroll slowly along the road. Everyone checks everyone else out, and sometimes love blooms!

Keeping up appearances

In the animal kingdom, keeping up appearances is a question of life or death. If you look good, you signify to potential mates that you are fit and healthy – and therefore have excellent genes to pass on to your offspring. Animals that look unkempt or unhealthy may be singled out by passing predators as weaklings – and possibly lunch.

FEEL-GOOD FACTOR

Research shows that attractive people are more likely to get good jobs, earn higher salaries, get off with lighter sentences if convicted of crimes and receive better care from their doctors. But don't panic: attractiveness is less about a perfect face and more about confidence, keeping eye contact, smiling and standing up straight.

Many teens find they are easily embarrassed and blush readily. Try to have confidence in everything you say and do.

Look Good, Feel Good

A messy room can quickly become a hovel with dirty bed linen, filthy clothes strewn on the floor and mouldering lumps of food scattered around.

Crash pad

If you invited someone to step into your bedroom, what is the first impression they would get? Just as your clothes and appearance say something about you, so does the space you keep for sleeping, working and chilling. Most of the time, your space probably says nothing more than 'quite busy, so can't be bothered with boring stuff like cleaning and tidying'.

When the pressure is on to do a massive clear out – you have a friend coming over, or your parents threaten to call in pest control – follow these simple steps for a sweet-smelling five-minute makeover.

DiD YOU KNOW?

Populations of blood-sucking bed bugs are on the increase in North America, Europe and Australia. They live in beds and dirty rooms, but can be prevented with good house hygiene.

1. *Draw your curtains and open a window.*
2. *Scoop all dirty clothes into a bin bag and tie it up so no odour can escape. Get it out of your room! Ideally, put dirty washing straight in the washing machine, or it will fester. Put smelly shoes outside.*
3. *Change your bed linen, but if there's no time just make your bed.*
4. *Remove all food.*
5. *Pick up everything else scattered around the room, put it in a cardboard box and hide it under the bed. If you have time, sort and tidy your stuff away.*
6. *Empty the bin, sweep the floor, or if you have a carpet, vacuum. If the carpet smells, sprinkle bicarbonate of soda (baking soda) over it, leave for a few minutes then vacuum: it soaks up smells.*
7. *Spray a little perfume or aftershave into the room.*

For the best results allow yourself more time: wash all your dirty clothes, air your duvet, pillows and mattress, dust and clean every surface.

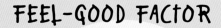

FEEL-GOOD FACTOR

If you suffer from allergies, eczema or asthma, you could find that keeping your clothes clean, and your living space free of dust – which is mostly dead skin – really helps. It is not just dust that irritates humans, so does the faeces (waste) of the billions of dust mites that feed on dead skin.

Laundry blues

Everyone gets the dirty laundry blues from time to time: you're going out, there is only one outfit you could possibly wear, and it's dirty. Using a washing machine isn't rocket science. Ask someone to show you how, and follow the fabric care symbols. Most machines have a 'quick-wash' programme. If time is short, try a rinse and spin cycle – or dab off any stains, spray the whole thing with water, so it is damp, not wet, and chuck it in the dryer (check the care labels first though), or hang it outside.

- Creased clothes can be smoothed by ironing, or by hanging them in the bathroom while you shower; the steam removes the creases.
- Get yourself a laundry basket and throw your dirty clothes in there, rather than on the floor. This will cut down nasty smells, and reduce dust.
- Underwear, t-shirts and socks should be washed after each wear, but you can just hang up other clothes (if they are clean and smell fresh) so they are ready for next time.

Before washing your clothes, check the care labels to make sure you're using the right cycle.

All Change

Puberty is the time when human bodies change from childhood to adulthood. It isn't marked by one single change, but a whole collection of transformations.

What controls puberty?

Your brain contains two control centres: the hypothalamus and the pituitary. They are glands that produce chemical messengers called hormones. No one is sure what triggers the beginning of puberty, but scientists have discovered a gene that starts the production of a hormone called Neurokin B in the hypothalamus. It triggers the production of gonadotrophin-releasing hormones, or GnRH, which travel to the pituitary gland. The pituitary gland, which sits below the brain, then produces more hormones that move through the bloodstream to the sex glands (ovaries in girls, testes in boys), and triggers puberty.

During puberty, boys' bodies change in several ways – hair starts to sprout, the voice breaks and they experience a growth spurt.

Puberty in boys

The testes are inside the testicles and they are the male sex glands. Testes make testosterone – the main male sex hormone that affects how your body and your brain develop, and is behind your interest in sex. Males have 10 times as much testosterone as females. The timing and order of these changes is different for everyone – and the whole process takes years.

TESTOSTERONE

Testosterone is a powerful hormone that acts on your brain and your body. Levels of testosterone fluctuate through the day, dropping lowest at midday. When levels are high, testosterone can make you more aggressive, angry, energetic and interested in sex.

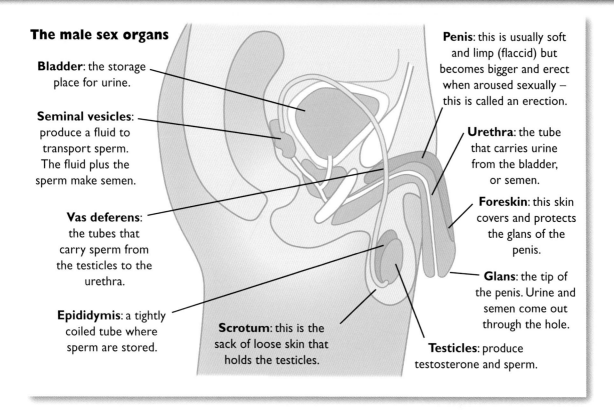

The male sex organs

Bladder: the storage place for urine.

Seminal vesicles: produce a fluid to transport sperm. The fluid plus the sperm make semen.

Vas deferens: the tubes that carry sperm from the testicles to the urethra.

Epididymis: a tightly coiled tube where sperm are stored.

Scrotum: this is the sack of loose skin that holds the testicles.

Penis: this is usually soft and limp (flaccid) but becomes bigger and erect when aroused sexually – this is called an erection.

Urethra: the tube that carries urine from the bladder, or semen.

Foreskin: this skin covers and protects the glans of the penis.

Glans: the tip of the penis. Urine and semen come out through the hole.

Testicles: produce testosterone and sperm.

What happens where?

- Brain: testosterone can make you more aggressive, emotional and sexually attracted to other people.
- Genitals: the penis, testicles and scrotum grow. The testicles start to produce sperm and the scrotum darkens. Pubic hair grows.
- Armpits: produce more sweat and hair grows.
- Nipples: may become temporarily swollen and sore.
- Face: hair grows, skin coarsens, jaw widens, spots usually appear.
- Arms and legs: become hairy, grow longer and muscles develop.
- Shoulders and chest: muscles grow, hair may appear.

- Adam's apple: gets bigger and voice breaks.
- Hair: can get oily or change in texture.
- Height and weight increase from growth spurt.

What's normal?

One of your greatest health concerns at the moment may be about whether your body is normal. Boys usually worry about when they will start growing, get hair and their voices will break. Everything is probably changing just the way it should. Penis size and shape is another common concern – but normal penises are all sorts of sizes and shapes, and your penis won't stop growing until you are aged 18 to 21.

DiD YOU KNOW?

You may wonder why testicles are in such a vulnerable position, hanging outside the body, but they are there for a good reason: sperm needs to be kept cool.

All Change

Infections and irritations

Male genitals are warm and often damp, sweaty places, so it's no wonder that infections develop there. Jock itch is an itchy, scaly rash that is caused by a fungus, and thrush is a yeast infection that causes itching and a smelly discharge from the penis. Both of these conditions can be prevented by following a good hygiene routine and wearing loose cotton underwear. Jock itch can be spread by sharing contaminated clothing and towels. A doctor can diagnose the conditions, and prescribe the best medication to treat them.

Keep it clean!

You may notice a white or yellow substance, called smegma, collecting under your foreskin. Your penis produces this substance naturally, but it can become a haven for bacteria, causing irritation and an unpleasant smell.

Washing properly is important for avoiding infections in warm, damp areas of your skin such as the genitals.

FEEL-GOOD FACTOR

There are lots of great websites and books about puberty that have been especially developed for teenagers. If you have any worries or anxieties, and feel too embarrassed to talk to someone about them, check out the Internet or the library for more information.

Washing your penis daily will prevent a build-up of smegma: gently pull back your foreskin and wash your penis when you shower or bath. Return your foreskin to its normal position. If your foreskin becomes red and sore, or is too tight to pull back, you will need to see a doctor.

Dealing with erections

A penis needs to be erect for sexual intercourse and ejaculation to occur. However, erections happen at other times too, especially if you are thinking about sex. During an erection, blood pumps into the penis, making it expand and go hard.

If you have an erection but don't ejaculate you may get an aching feeling in your testicles. Sometimes, your body takes over and causes an ejaculation you weren't even aware of, particularly in your sleep. This is a wet dream, and you will know you've had one when you wake and find your sheets are damp. It's time to get familiar with the workings of a washing machine when this happens!

You can give yourself an erection, and an orgasm, by masturbating – which means giving yourself sexual pleasure by touching or rubbing your genitals. Masturbation is a normal and natural activity for males and females.

Lumps and bumps

You may find small lumps or bumps on your penis. These are very common and are usually sebaceous glands or spots. They are harmless and you should not try to pick them. However, if

In the Jewish religion, all baby boys are circumcised in a ceremony known as a bris.

> ## DiD YOU KNOW?
>
> *Circumcision is the removal of a boy's foreskin; it is sometimes carried out for religious reasons, or because people think it is more hygienic. Some men say that circumcision reduces their ability to enjoy sex.*

you are sexually active, you may have caught an infection, and should see a doctor.

Lumps around the genital area, upper thighs and belly may be caused by hernias. Hernias occur when a weakness in layers of muscle allows part of an organ, such as the intestines, to poke through, creating a lump. They can take a long time to develop, or can occur suddenly, after lifting heavy weights or straining on the toilet. If you think you have a hernia you should consult a doctor, as they can suddenly become medical emergencies.

All Change

You may find that your friends develop earlier than you; their breasts may grow and they may start their periods. Don't worry – you'll catch up!

Puberty in girls

Girls' ovaries produce oestrogen – the main female sex hormone that affects how your body and your brain develop. As with boys, the way your body changes, and the time puberty takes, vary from one girl to the next.

What happens where?

- Brain: oestrogen affects your moods and emotions.
- Genitals: hair grows around the pubic area and your external sex organs get slightly bigger.
- Armpits: produce more sweat and hair grows.

DiD YOU KNOW?

You were born with around two million eggs in your ovaries, but only around 400 of these will become fully mature through your lifetime.

- Face and hair: can become oily and spots usually appear.
- Hips and thighs broaden and healthy layers of fat are laid down to produce a womanly figure.
- Nipples and breasts grow; one side often starts growing before the other and it's normal to have one breast larger than the other.
- Inside your body, your sex organs mature and prepare for their role in reproduction. The first signs of this are a white or cream discharge from your vagina, and the beginning of periods.

The female sex organs

Uterus: this is the place where babies grow. It is also known as a womb.

Clitoris: this is a mound of fleshy skin that is the size of pea. It is full of nerves, and is the place where women can feel most sexual pleasure.

Fallopian tubes: eggs travel down these to the uterus.

Ovary: there are two of these. They produce eggs.

Uterine lining: this is shed, and passes through the vagina, when girls have their monthly periods.

Vulva: the parts of a female's genitals that can be seen outside her body.

Cervix: a small opening at the neck of the uterus. It widens when a baby is being born.

Labia: flaps of skin that cover the genital openings that grow and may darken during puberty.

Urethra: the hole through which urine flows.

Vaginal opening: this is the opening that a penis enters during sex, and where babies come out when they are born.

Vagina: the stretchy tube that leads to the cervix and uterus. Also known as the birth canal, because this is the route babies follow when they are born.

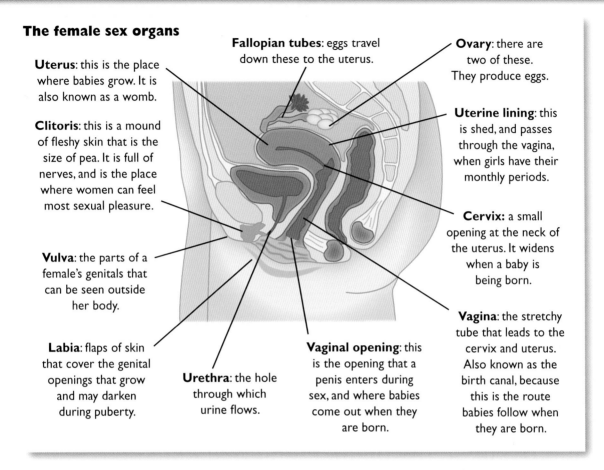

What's normal?

You may wonder whether all the things that are happening to your body are normal. Many new feelings, aches and pains are natural; for example, breasts can become tender or even a bit lumpy around the time of a period. Aching bones and sore muscles can also accompany sudden growth spurts.

For girls, one of the biggest concerns about puberty is having periods. Until your periods begin, you don't know what to expect – and then once they have started you discover they can be unpredictable, painful and a bit messy! The trick to dealing with periods is to be prepared for them, and to learn how to keep their impact to a minimum.

FEEL-GOOD FACTOR

Weight gain is normal for girls going through puberty; growing a curvy figure and laying down fat on your thighs and hips is natural. It is your body's way of preparing you for future motherhood, when these stores of food will help with the high-energy demands of pregnancy and breast-feeding.

Make a note in a diary of when your period is due – that way you'll be prepared.

Cramps in the lower belly often accompany periods. Taking exercise can reduce the pain, but if you can't face moving try painkillers and a hot water bottle.

Towels and tampons

Periods often appear unannounced, although as you get older you will learn to recognise the warning signs that your period is due, and can prepare for it. Periods are more like a leak than a gush, so it's unlikely anyone else will know if you do get caught out, but using panty liners is a good, cheap way to catch the first stages of a period if you are worried about it.

Women use sanitary towels (STs) and tampons to protect their clothes during periods. It is important that STs and tampons are changed regularly, and are wrapped up before being thrown away. Sanitary towels are absorbent pads that stick to your knickers. They come in different sizes and absorbencies, as you might need greater absorbency for part of your period, and at night. You can't wear STs when you go swimming. Tampons are made from absorbent material and are inserted into the vagina, either with your hands or a special applicator. You pull a tampon out using the string attached to the tampon. You should read the instructions carefully and wash your hands before using tampons to avoid the risk of getting Toxic Shock Syndrome.

Periods

Periods are part of a woman's natural menstrual cycle, when the lining of the uterus thickens to prepare for a possible baby. When there is no baby, the uterus lining breaks up and passes out of the vagina, with some blood – this is a 'period'.

- A period may last anything from a few days to eight or more.
- Periods occur around every 28 days, but each woman's cycle is different.
- Periods may be very irregular and heavy, especially for the first year or so.
- You can miss a period if you are ill or anxious.

FEEL-GOOD FACTOR

Periods can feel like they are taking over your life for a few days. Your hormones may make you more emotional just before a period – this is known as premenstrual syndrome, or PMS. Thankfully, chocolate has iron, calcium and magnesium – three minerals that may help your body cope with PMS!

There is no need to use special soaps or vaginal sprays when you are having a period; normal washing is fine. In fact, some products can remove the vagina's natural defences, allowing infections to develop.

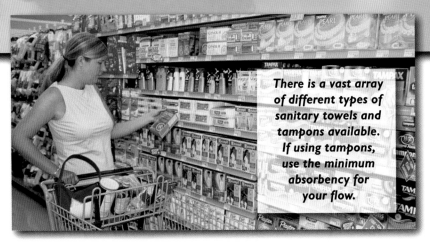

There is a vast array of different types of sanitary towels and tampons available. If using tampons, use the minimum absorbency for your flow.

Toxic Shock Syndrome

Toxic Shock Syndrome (TSS) is a medical condition that can occur when bacteria grow on a tampon that's being used. Symptoms include sudden high fever, headache, a rash and dizziness. TSS is a rare but extremely serious condition. To avoid the risk of getting TSS, always wash your hands properly before and after handling a tampon, use the lowest absorbency you need, change your tampons every four to six hours and alternate tampons with sanitary towels.

Thrush

Thrush is a burning, itching infection that is caused by a sudden growth of naturally occurring yeast around the vagina. It is often accompanied by a thick, smelly discharge. Most women get thrush at some time in their lives but it can be easily treated using medications available from pharmacies. Thrush can be caused by antibiotics, tight clothing, soap and bubble baths, vaginal deodorants, or from trying to wash inside your vagina (you don't need to – it's self-cleaning).

If menstrual blood leaks onto your underwear or bedding, it is best to remove it quickly, before it dries. Soak the fabric in cold water, preferably with biological powder, before washing it.

Relationships

We all rely on our relationships. Friends and family are an essential part of our well-being and often bring us great joy and comfort. But building and keeping those relationships can be tough.

Feelings

The racing hormones of puberty do not just affect your body; they also change your brain. Levels of sex hormones continually fluctuate, causing surges of different emotions in a very short time, from anger and aggression to sadness and depression. Add to this chemical mix social, physical and educational pressures – and it's no wonder your emotions are all over the place.

Arrows of desire

In ancient Greece, Eros was honoured as the god of love. (He was known as Cupid by the Romans, since 'cupido' means 'desire'.) Shown as a young winged boy and armed with a bow, Eros shot golden arrows with dove feathers into the hearts of people, making them feel love. He shot leaden arrows with owl feathers to spread indifference.

If you have ever fallen for someone, you'll know the feeling of being shot in the heart – it's overwhelming.

In adolescence, these passionate feelings are often called crushes, especially if the feelings of desire are directed towards someone you don't know very well, such as a teacher, or someone you don't actually know at all – like a singer, actor or model.

The painful thing about crushes is that they are mostly unrequited – your feelings are not returned. Crushes can dominate your thoughts, and are often tied up with unrealistic hopes about where your passion could lead. If your crush is for

During puberty, your hormones will be racing. You'll find yourself thinking about love – and sex – more than ever.

Many teens have crushes on people of the same sex, but this doesn't necessarily mean they are gay – sexuality is still developing during adolescence.

someone you know, and who is a similar age to you, then you may have a chance at real romance, but be prepared for a possible let-down – Eros is busy shooting as many leaden arrows as he is shooting those lovely golden ones!

Crushes are normal, and usually short-lived, but if you are obsessed with thoughts of someone, or can't shake off the distress of rejection, talk to your friends and ask them to help you find other interests to distract you.

Straight or gay?

The years of adolescence are largely concerned with sexuality – developing bodies that are ready for sex, discovering one's sexuality and preparing for healthy, happy sex lives as adults. During this process you may question whether

DiD YOU KNOW?

Being gay or straight is not a choice people make, and your sexuality is not something you can change – it's just the way you are. However, in some societies, gay people are treated as criminals.

HOMOSEXUALITY

Homosexuality is widespread in nature. Young male dolphins, for example, often pair up in sexual partnerships, and nearly all bonobos – apes that are closely related to chimps – are bisexual. They use sex to resolve conflicts and are known as the 'make love, not war' apes!

you are gay or straight. Confused? Here are some useful facts about sexuality:

• Heterosexual ('straight') means having sexual feelings for people of the opposite sex.
• Homosexual ('gay') means having sexual feelings for people of the same sex.
• A lesbian is a gay woman.
• Bisexual means having sexual feelings for people of both sexes.
• Some people only discover they are gay in their teens or as adults.

Relationships

Enjoy getting to know your partner before you decide to become more intimate with each other.

OXYTOCIN

Oxytocin is known as the 'love hormone'. It is made by the hypothalamus and it helps people form bonds with one another by increasing the amount they trust and care for one another. It seems to play a part in falling in love, and staying together for a long time.

Dating

Dating is like on-the-job training. It's the way we all learn how to make relationships work, and discover what personalities we get on with. The first stage of dating is usually friendship, and that leads to 'going out', if you fancy each other. Sometimes, it's tough to know whether someone you fancy feels the same way back, so it's wise to be prepared for rejection. This is the point when your friends and family will remind you that 'there are plenty more fish in the sea'! They're right of course, but it can still knock your confidence for a while.

When you've dated someone for a little while, you may want to get more intimate with him or her. Taking a relationship to the next stage often happens naturally so there is no time to prepare for it. However, you should always be sure that kissing or touching each other is something you both want to do.

Parents – what's it got to do with them?

It is your parents' job to keep you happy and safe, and they will never really stop feeling this responsibility – even when you are grown-up with kids of your own. So don't be surprised if they're interested in your relationships – most of the time they just want to protect you from getting hurt or making mistakes.

Keep parents on-side by telling them who you are dating, and how things are going. They are more likely to allow you greater freedom if they know they can trust you – and your boyfriend or girlfriend – and if they feel confident that you will ask them for help and advice when you need it.

FEEL-GOOD FACTOR

A broken heart hurts terribly, but it's something we all need to go through, especially as teens, in order to learn how to love as adults. The poet Byron wrote, 'Like the measles, love is most dangerous when it comes late in life.' Your heartache will help you learn to be a kinder, more sympathetic adult.

It can feel lonely being single, but try spending time with friends or starting a new hobby. There's no need to feel left out.

Being single

Not everyone is dating all the time. Some teens choose not to date, others haven't found someone to go out with and others are purposefully taking some time out of the dating scene. Whatever the reason, here are some top tips to help you get the most out of singledom:

1. When you are in a relationship, keep investing time and energy into your friendships, so your friends will be there for you when you are single.
2. The best relationships bloom from friendship, so seek out new ways to make friends. Investigate clubs that are available through school, or church etc.
3. Let people down kindly if you don't want to go out with them.
4. Keep a balance in your life. Your school work is important, but it is best to keep up with other interests too, such as sports and hobbies.
5. If you are feeling unwanted, take care of your self-esteem. Remind yourself of your good qualities, and know that your family and friends all think you're great.

REAL LIFE

'I finished with my boyfriend when I found out he was two-timing me. I was devastated and I didn't think I would get over the hurt. My mates were so supportive. They took me out, cheered me up – that really helped.'
Melissa (15)

Relationships

Choices about sex

Sex is a powerful topic that stirs up lots of feelings and beliefs. For a few people, sex is just a physical activity like any other. But for most of us, sex is about much more, because it involves your mind and heart as well as your body. Emotions of passion, desire, love, pleasure, trust, intimacy and honesty all play a part in good sex.

Deciding when, and if, you are ready for sex depends on lots of things. This is what some teens said about sex:

'I felt sex was a hurdle I just had to get over. I lost my virginity as soon as I could.'

'I don't want to have sex yet. I think I'd get it all wrong. It frightens me.'

'I love my boyfriend, and making love is a natural part of that. But I haven't told my parents we sleep together.'

'Once you've started having sex, it's much harder to make a new partner wait until you're ready.'

'I am saving myself for marriage. I believe sex should be about making love, and it is sacred.'

What do you think about these comments? Do you agree with any of them? If not, what are your reasons?

Kissing your partner is one thing, but make sure you don't get carried away unless you're both comfortable taking the next step.

DiD YOU KNOW?

You are more likely to start having sex if you think your friends are already having sex, even though many of them are probably lying!

Setting boundaries

What do we mean by 'having sex'? Some people are happy to engage in very intimate sexual activities with a partner, but if they don't have full intercourse, they don't think it is sex.

Here are some expressions you may have heard:

• Petting. This means touching for pleasure e.g. kissing and touching each other, especially around the genitals.
• Mutual masturbation. This means giving each other sexual pleasure by touching each other's genitals, usually using your hands or mouth.
• Sexual intercourse. This is when the penis goes into the vagina.
• Virgin. This is a person who has not had sexual intercourse.

If you are in a relationship it is important to know how far you are prepared to go, to tell your partner what your boundaries are, and to discover what limits they may want to set. Sex involves lots of talking and being honest with one another. If you are being physically intimate with someone else and they ask you to stop, you must respect their wishes – if you don't, you could be guilty of sexual abuse or rape. If you decide you are unhappy with any physical intimacy with someone, you have every right to ask them to stop at any time.

FEEL-GOOD FACTOR

If you're thinking about moving your relationship
on a step, ask yourselves these questions:
• What do we want from this relationship?
• Are we ready?
• Are we committed to each other?
• What are our feelings towards each other?
• How will be keep ourselves safe and protected?

If you're not comfortable
talking to your partner
about sex, you probably
aren't ready to actually do it.

Pregnancy and Contraception

Once puberty begins, your body is preparing for parenthood. Contraception, or birth control, is the variety of methods used to prevent pregnancy.

A repro recap

You already know the ultimate point of sex is to make babies. You've probably been taught about the birds and bees – or 'facts of life' but here's a reminder:

1. When a man becomes sexually aroused, his penis becomes stiff and erect. When a woman become aroused, blood flows to her genitals and her vagina becomes moist.

2. The man puts his penis into his partner's vagina, which expands to make room. The couple move their hips so the penis rubs against the vaginal walls. This gives them both pleasure, and leads to the man ejaculating (this is an orgasm, or climax).

3. During ejaculation, millions of sperm enter the vagina and travel to the fallopian tubes. If an egg is there, one sperm may penetrate its outer membrane and fertilise the egg.

4. A fertilised egg settles in the uterus, ready to start growing into an embryo, which will eventually become a baby.

5. Pregnancy lasts around nine months. The mother's body protects the growing baby, which gets its nourishment from her through a placenta. At the end of the pregnancy, the baby is born, emerging through the vagina.

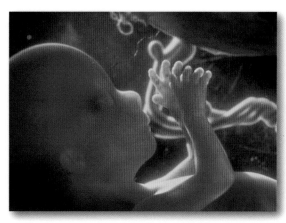

By four months, an unborn child has human features and is developing rapidly.

Myths about pregnancy

'If you have sex standing up, the sperm can't reach the egg.' Sperm stay alive for up to five days, so unless you are planning on keeping your fingers crossed and standing for a long time…

'If you use it right, contraception always works.' There is no method of contraception that is 100 per cent perfect. If you have sex, even with contraception, there is a chance of pregnancy.

'You can't get a girl pregnant if you withdraw your penis before ejaculating.' Yes you can: some sperm sneak out of your penis before ejaculation.

'You won't get pregnant if you don't have sex.' Sperm can make their way from the vulva into the vagina and onwards to find an egg. So even a virgin can get pregnant.

'If you have sex before your first period you can't get pregnant.' You produce an egg before your first period, so you could be fertile.

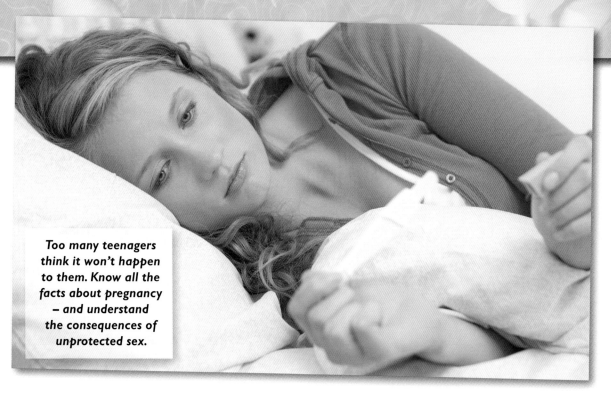

Too many teenagers think it won't happen to them. Know all the facts about pregnancy – and understand the consequences of unprotected sex.

The end of a pregnancy

Some pregnancies come to an early end because either the mother's body cannot maintain the pregnancy, or there is something wrong with the growing embryo; this is called a miscarriage.

Some women choose to terminate their pregnancies. This brings about the death of the embryo and it is called an abortion, or termination. It is achieved by taking medication (the 'abortion pill') in the very early stages of pregnancy, or by a surgical procedure that removes the growing embryo.

Your doctor will be able to answer any questions you may have about contraception or terminating a pregnancy.

DiD YOU KNOW?

Around 250 million sperm are propelled out of the male body during an ejaculation. Sperm can live outside the body for up to four hours and can even be transferred to the vagina on your hands.

PREGNANCY TESTING

For most women, the first sign of a pregnancy is missing a period. Pregnancy tests are available from pharmacies and they are most accurate about one week after the first day of a missed period. If a woman gets a positive result, she should see her doctor.

Pregnancy and Contraception

Condoms are usually available in pharmacies, supermarkets and many other outlets. You may also be able to get them from a walk-in clinic.

Choosing contraception

If you are sexually active, or think there is any chance you may become sexually active soon you need to think about contraception – even if you do not plan to have full sexual intercourse.

There are many types of contraceptive available. Of these, the easiest to get hold of are condoms, which you can buy from many shops, including pharmacies and supermarkets. Other methods of contraception are available through your doctor, a family-planning centre or a sexual-health clinic – they may have side effects and long-term implications for your health, so you need a medical professional's help to decide which one is best for you.

No method of contraception is 100 per cent guaranteed, but if you use contraception properly it is much more likely to work effectively.

Condoms

Condoms have been around for hundreds of years, and were originally made from animal membranes. Thankfully, modern ones are made from ultra-thin but tough synthetic materials, such as latex and polyurethane.

Also known as sheaths, condoms are unrolled on to an erect penis. They work by catching the semen in a teat at the end. They must be carefully removed after use, to make sure none of the semen leaks out. Female condoms have been invented too. They line the inside of the vagina, but they are more expensive than male condoms and can be tricky to use properly.

Condoms are not only good at stopping pregnancies, they also prevent many sexually transmitted infections (STIs, see page 40).

The pill

The contraceptive pill, known as 'the pill', has been in widespread use since the 1960s. Each pill contains hormones that affect a woman's body, either stopping ovulation (the production of an egg) or preventing a fertilised egg from implanting in the uterus and making it harder for sperm to reach an egg.

A woman who is on the pill takes one pill a day every day, or for three weeks out of four. The pill is very effective as long as it is used according to the instructions. Vomiting or diarrhoea can stop it from working for the rest of the woman's cycle. The pill does not protect against sexually transmitted infections.

Sterilisation

When a person is sterilised the aim is to prevent them from being able to have children.

STAYING SAFE

Condoms have a 'use by' date. The packet should be intact, and in good condition. Using oil-based creams or lubricants (like Vaseline) with a condom can damage it. Handle condoms carefully, as they tear easily. Never use a condom more than once.

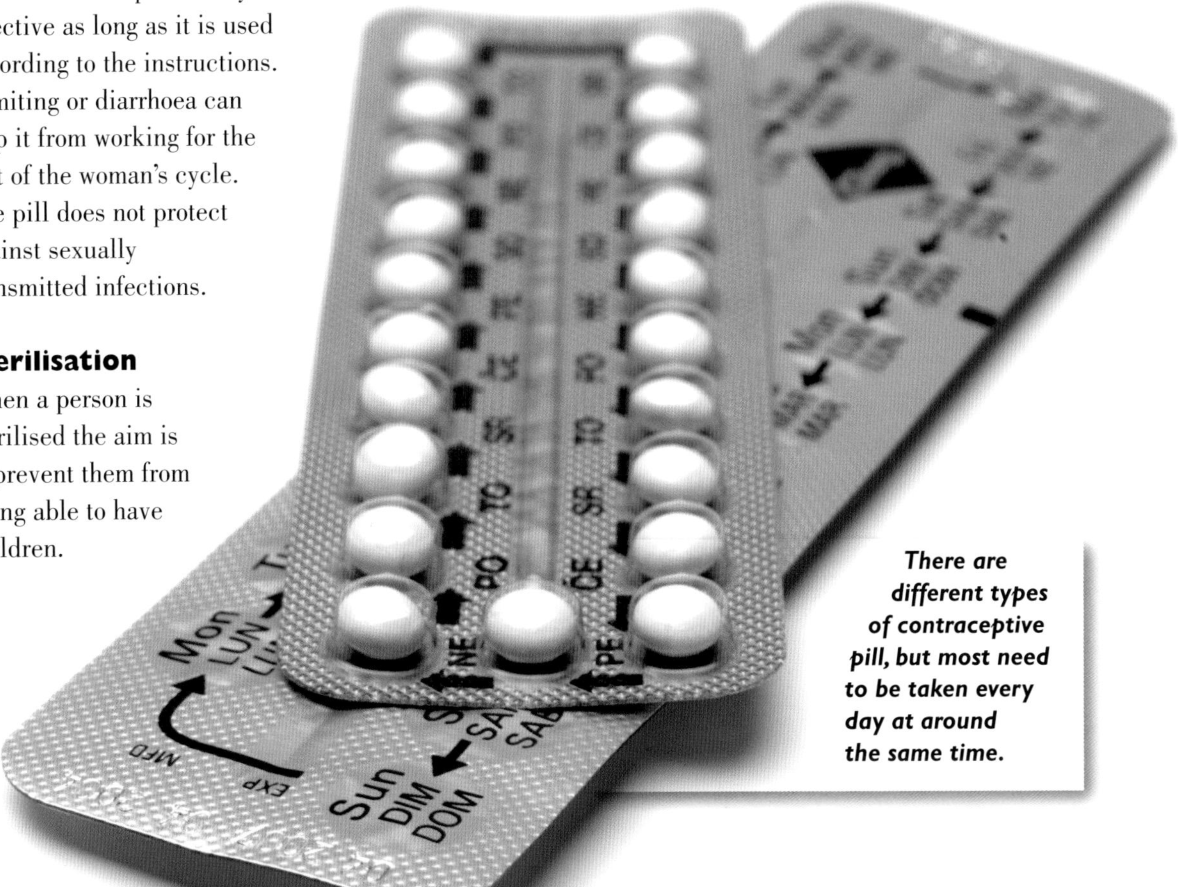

Sterilisation in a man is called a vasectomy and it involves the cutting or blocking of the tubes (vas deferens) that carry sperm. Sterilisation in a woman usually involves an operation to cut or block the fallopian tubes. Since sterilisation is a permanent method of contraception, it is normally only carried out once adults have completed their families.

There are different types of contraceptive pill, but most need to be taken every day at around the same time.

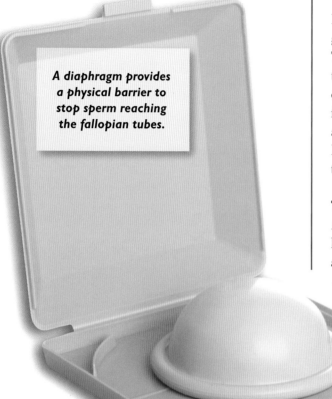

A diaphragm provides a physical barrier to stop sperm reaching the fallopian tubes.

The IUD

Intra-uterine devices, or IUDs, are small gadgets that are put into a woman's uterus. They work by stopping the uterus lining from thickening (so embryos cannot implant there), or by preventing sperm from reaching a fertile egg. Doctors insert IUDs, and they are usually left in place for around five years. IUDs give no protection against sexually transmitted infections.

The diaphragm

A diaphragm is made from cup-shaped soft latex and it fits over a woman's cervix. When a woman is planning to have intercourse, she applies spermicidal cream to the diaphragm, and inserts it into her vagina. Diaphragms can be quite tricky to use properly, and they do not protect against STIs. You need a doctor to fit the correct size of diaphragm for you, and to show you how to use it.

Injections and implants

Contraceptive injections of hormones for women only need to be given every three months, and they are very effective at preventing pregnancy. Unfortunately they weaken bones, so they are only prescribed for teens who have difficulty using any other type of contraception.

Hormone implants are the size of a thin matchstick and they are inserted under a woman's skin, where they release hormones for several years. They are very effective at preventing pregnancy, but very few doctors have been trained in inserting them. They are a new method of contraception, so their long-term effects are not fully known yet. Injections and implants do not protect you against STIs.

FEEL-GOOD FACTOR

In some countries, including the UK and the USA, advice about contraception and contraceptives is free to young people. Advice is given in confidence, so you do not need to tell your parents. However, it is a good idea to discuss contraception with your parents, if you feel you can.

Spermicides

As you might guess from their name, spermicides kill sperm. They are also known as chemical contraceptives. They can be used as creams, or foams, tablets or sponges, and are inserted into the vagina. No spermicides should be used alone, as there is a chance that some sperm will survive, but they can be used with condoms for extra protection. Spermicides can be bought from pharmacies without a prescription. They do not protect against STIs.

The emergency pill

The emergency pill, or 'morning-after pill' is a type of contraception that can be used after unprotected intercourse, or if contraception fails, e.g. if a condom splits during use. It works in a variety of ways, depending on where the woman is in her menstrual cycle: it can stop a fertilised egg from being released, it can stop sperm reaching an egg and it can also prevent a fertilised egg from implanting in the uterus.

The emergency pill only works for up to 72 hours after unprotected sex, and it is more effective the sooner it is taken. You may be able to buy it from a pharmacy, or you can get it from your doctor or a family-planning clinic. It should only be used in emergencies, not as regular contraception, and it does not protect against STIs.

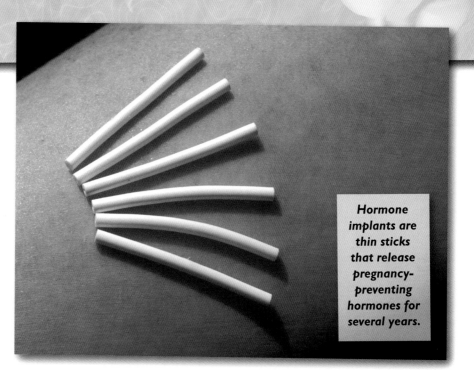

Hormone implants are thin sticks that release pregnancy-preventing hormones for several years.

You can get emergency contraception from your pharmacist, who will advise you on how to take it.

DiD YOU KNOW?

Contraception is not a new idea. Women of ancient times put lumps of crocodile dung, or sponges soaked in vinegar, into their vaginas to stop or kill sperm.

Staying Healthy

As you move into adulthood, keeping healthy gets more complicated. Intimate relationships can leave you exposed to certain infections and diseases; equip yourself with the know-how to avoid them, and stay safe.

Sexually transmitted infections

Sexually transmitted infections (STIs) are sometimes called sexually transmitted diseases (STDs). They used to be called venereal diseases (VD).

Anyone who has sexual contact with another person may get an STI, but some of them are becoming particularly common amongst teens. It is important to take every step you can to avoid getting STIs because they not only affect your immediate health, they can cause you permanent damage – even death. Some STIs affect fertility, which means you might never be able to have a baby.

STIs Need to Know

- You can't tell if someone has an STI just by looking at their genitals.
- You can get an STI without having intercourse: skin-to-skin contact is sometimes enough.
- You could have an STI without knowing it, which means you might pass it on to anyone else.
- You can catch an STI from one partner, from having sex just once.

STIs – fancy one of these?

- Chlamydia. A widespread infection. Often has no symptoms, but can make a woman infertile.
- Genital herpes. Causes weeping blisters and sores around the genitals. The virus lives in your body forever and is contagious even when there are no sores.

Some STIs can be passed through tiny cuts or tears in the skin inside the mouth, so even kissing can put you at risk of an STI.

REAL LIFE

'My husband and I were trying to have a baby for a few years before the doctors found my fallopian tubes were damaged from an infection I never knew I had. It's unlikely I'll ever get pregnant.'
Megan (31)

This is a magnified image of a pubic louse. These 'crabs' spread through shared bedding and clothing, and through sexual contact.

- Genital warts. Causes warty bumps on the genitals. The virus can cause cervical cancer in women.
- Gonorrhoea. First symptoms, if you get any, include pain when you pee and a discharge (for males and females). May cause infertility, and can spread to other organs.
- Syphilis. Causes red sores, a rash and flu-like symptoms. Symptoms disappear, but the infection stays in the body and attacks the organs. Can cause death.
- Lice ('Crabs'). Pubic lice are blood-sucking parasites that live in pubic hair. They are extremely itchy.
- Hepatitis B. Symptoms, if you have any, include feeling unwell and a pain in the liver. Can damage your liver permanently, and can cause liver cancer.
- HIV. This virus is passed through body fluids, such as semen and blood. Causes AIDS, a life-threatening disease that destroys your immune system.

The ABC of safe sex

A: Abstain

This means either not having sex at all, or waiting until you are older. The younger you are when you start having sex, the greater your chances of catching an STI.

B: Be aware

The more sexual partners you have, the more likely you are to catch an STI, and pass it to others.

C: Condoms

Condoms are the only contraceptives that will cut down your chance of catching an STI, but they do not prevent all of them.

FEEL-GOOD FACTOR

Untreated STIs can cause Pelvic Inflammatory Disease (PID) in women – a condition that causes scarring in the reproductive system, leading to infertility. If you think there is any chance you have been in contact with an STI, get yourself checked out as soon as possible.

HIV/AIDS

More than 33 million people live with the HIV virus in the world, and 15 million children have been orphaned because of its deadly effects. There is currently no cure for HIV/AIDs, and no vaccination to prevent it. Safe sex, or no sex, are the best ways to avoid catching this terrible disease.

Staying Healthy

Taking responsibility for your own well-being means regular visits to healthcare professionals such as your optician and dentist.

Stay safe, stay well

Maintaining good health is not just about keeping yourself clear of infections. It is about your whole approach to following a healthy lifestyle; your body is the vessel that will carry you through life, and all of your experiences and achievements will be affected and influenced by your physical and mental health.

FEEL-GOOD FACTOR

Get to know your body. Find out what is normal for you, and then you will be able to identify any changes that may need medical attention. As you get older, you may be invited to attend screenings for conditions, such as cervical cancer or STIs.

Living with medical conditions

From asthma to heart disease, depression and diabetes, there are many lifelong medical conditions that affect young people. Coping with medications, treatments, therapies or hospital visits can be especially hard when you are in your teens, and you have so many more interesting and fun things to think about.

If you have to cope with a medical condition that affects your daily life, you may find it helpful to:
- Get into a routine for taking medications.
- Keep information about your medications.
- Learn about your condition, and how your medications are designed to help you.
- Think about the consequences of not looking after yourself.
- Learn how to take responsibility for your condition and its treatment, as you prepare for adulthood.

Health checklist

Taking responsibility for your own health means working towards preventing medical conditions or ill-health from ever developing, if you can.

In the last year have you:
- Had your eyesight checked?
- Been to the dentist?
- Checked you are up to date with all your vaccinations?
- Worn sunscreen whenever you have been in the sun?

A healthy lifestyle is all about balance. Make time for exercise and enjoy the company of your friends!

If you are sexually active, have you:

- Sought contraceptive advice?
- Always used contraception?
- Been checked out for STIs?

If you have a medical condition, have you:

- Had a review with your doctor, to make sure your treatment is still the best for your condition?
- Always made sure you follow your doctor's advice and recommendations for managing your health?

Do you:

- Visit a doctor when you have a medical problem?
- Eat a balanced, healthy diet?
- Avoid alcohol and drugs?
- Get a good night's sleep most nights?
- Take regular exercise?
- Get involved with sports activities?
- Put time into your friendships and family relationships?
- Talk to family and friends when you are anxious, depressed or worried?
- Support others around you when they need help?
- Know how and where to get help for any problem you may have?

REAL LIFE

'I was born premature, and have cerebral palsy as a result. It means I have trouble controlling my muscles and coordination. I've had speech therapy, physical therapy and surgery, but I try to lead as full and active a life as I can.'
Max (14)

Glossary

acne a skin condition that can cause spots and infections, often on the face, chest and back.

adolescence the time of development between the beginning of puberty and adulthood.

allergy extreme sensitivity to certain things, such as pollen.

antibiotics types of medication that kill bacteria and are used to treat bacterial infections.

anxiety a feeling of worry or tension.

asthma an illness that causes difficulty breathing.

cavity a hole in a tooth, caused by decay.

cerebral palsy a movement disorder caused by damage to the brain.

contraception methods used to prevent pregnancy.

depilatory cream a cream used to dissolve hair above the skin's surface.

depression an emotional state of gloom and deep sadness, or a medical condition characterised by the same emotions.

ejaculation when semen is pushed out of the penis during orgasm.

emollient a cream or lotion that softens the skin.

epilation a method of hair removal that involves pulling each hair out of the skin.

fertile a fertile person is able to reproduce. An infertile person is unlikely to become a mother or father without medical help.

gay attracted to people of the same sex.

genitals the body's external sex organs.

hepatitis a liver disease; there are several kinds.

hormones chemical messengers produced by glands in the body. Hormones are transported by the blood to instruct cells and organs to work in a particular way.

hypothalamus part of the brain that is a control centre for many functions, such as the production of hormones.

immune system the body's system that combats infections and diseases.

lesbian a gay, or homosexual, woman.

menstruation when the lining of the uterus passes from the body as blood, known as a period.

oestrogen the female hormone that controls puberty and some parts of the reproductive system.

orgasm the most intense point of pleasure experienced during sex.

orthodontics a branch of dentistry that corrects and straightens teeth.

puberty the time at the beginning of adolescence when the sex organs develop.

reproduction the process of making a new life.

retainer a small piece of orthodontic equipment that is moulded to the shape of your teeth and gums to preserve orthodontic corrections.

sebaceous glands glands in the skin that produce sebum, an oily substance.

stress an emotional feeling of strain, tension or anxiety and a physical state of the body.

stretch marks fine lines that appear in the skin when it has been stretched. They are often caused by growth spurts or pregnancy and are common on the belly, thighs, buttocks, breasts and back.

testosterone the sex hormone that controls some aspects of male puberty and the male reproductive system.

tetanus a life-threatening bacterial disease.

Further Information

Books

Diary of a Teenage Health Freak
by Ann McPherson and Aidan Macfarlane
(Oxford University Press, 2002)

*Do the Right Thing: A Teenager's Survival Guide
for Tricky Situations*
by Jane Goldman
(Piccadilly Press, 2007)

*Girls Only! All About Periods and
Growing Up Stuff*
by Victoria Parker
(Hodder Children's Books, 2004)

*Sex, Puberty and All That Stuff –
a Guide to Growing Up*
by Jacqui Bailey
(Franklin Watts, 2005)

*Taking Responsibility: A Teen's Guide
to Contraception and Pregnancy*
by Donna Lange
(Mason Crest Publishers, 2004)

The Truth, A Teenager's Survival Guide
by Ann McPherson & Aidan Macfarlane
(Oxford University Press, 2007)

Websites

http://www.ru-ok.org.uk
The RU-OK website offers advice on a range of
issues, helping teenagers to help themselves.

http://www.connexions-direct.com
The Connexions Direct website is aimed
at teenagers with information on health,
relationships, careers, learning, money and
a whole lot more.

http://www.teenissues.co.uk
This website covers every teen issue
imaginable, from how to deal with step-families
to keeping up to date with current events.
There is also a forum where you can ask
experts for advice.

http://www.teenagehealthfreak.org
The extensive index on this site will lead you
to articles on all manner of teen health issues,
including sexual health.

Index